A BOOK OF WORDS THAT SOUND THE SAME

The lonely ***pear***

makes a ***pair.***

The little ***fly***

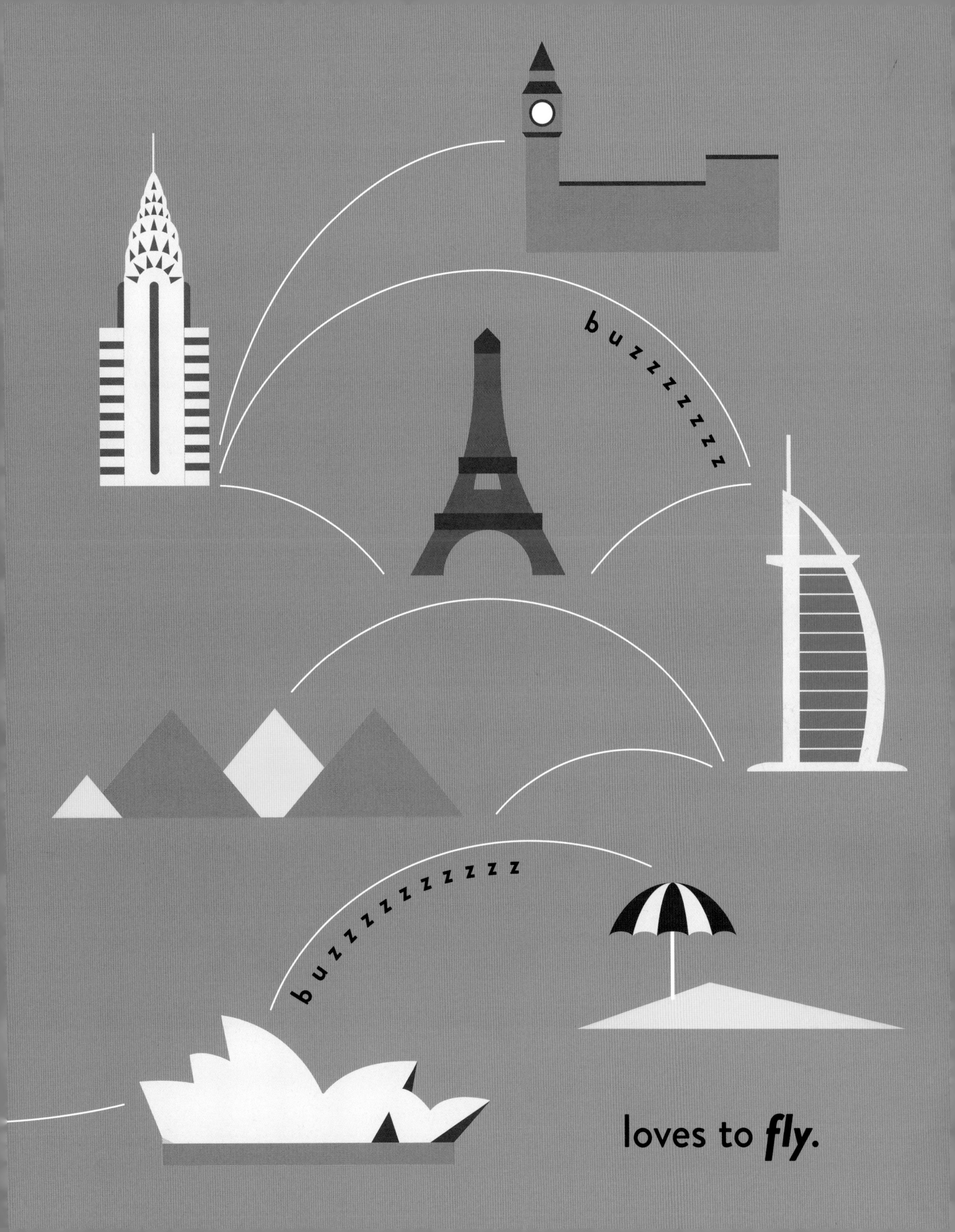
buzzzzzzz
buzzzzzzzzzz

loves to ***fly.***

The stylish ***hare***

has great ***hair***.

The tall ***duck***

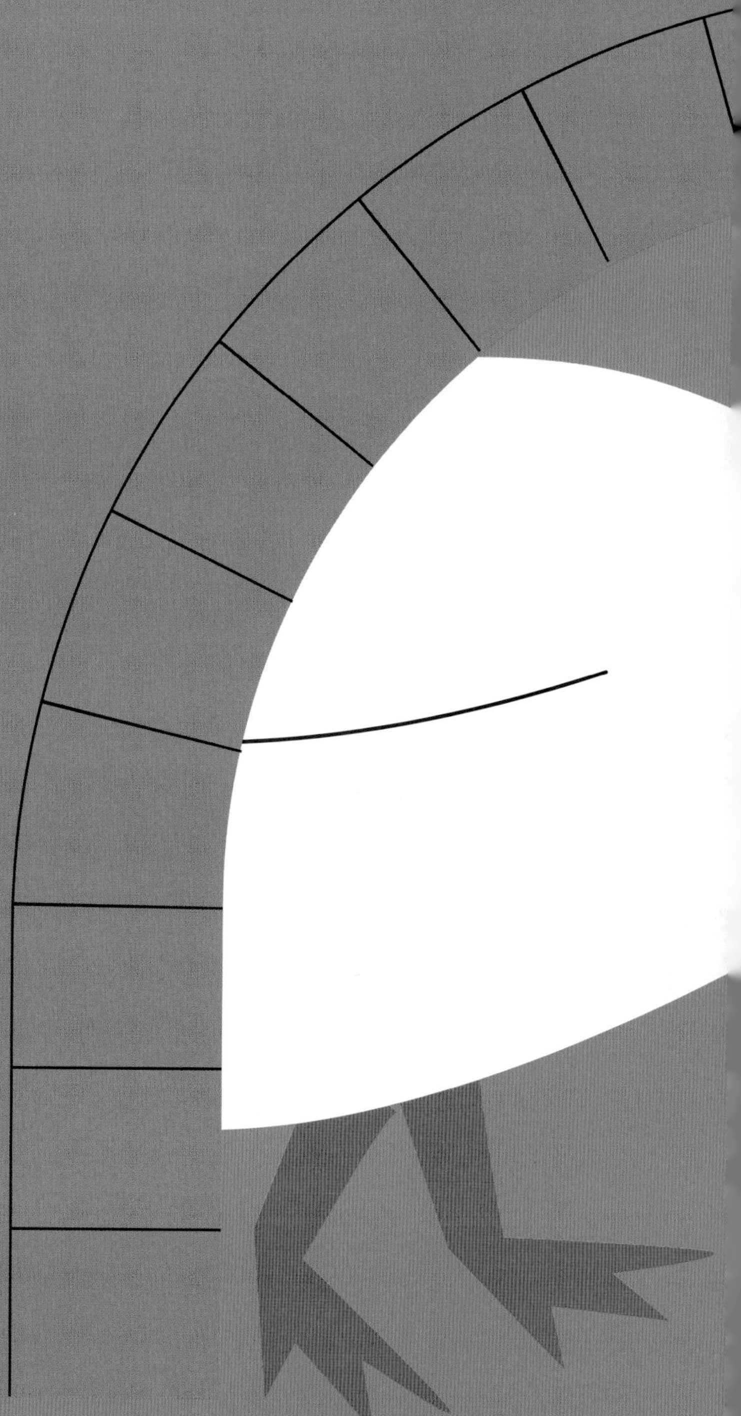

has to ***duck***.

"Oh **dear**!"

says the ***deer.***

The lazy ***toad***

likes to be **towed.**

The ***knight***

is out of sight at ***night***.

The lazy ***boar***

is a ***bore.***
Z
Z
Z
Z
z

The poor ***horse***

is rather **hoarse.**
SNEEZE!
ATCHOO!
COUGH!

The cats ***pause***

to lick their ***paws.***

The boy **waves**

on the ocean **waves.**

The sad ***whale***

is having a ***wail***.

The curious ***crane***

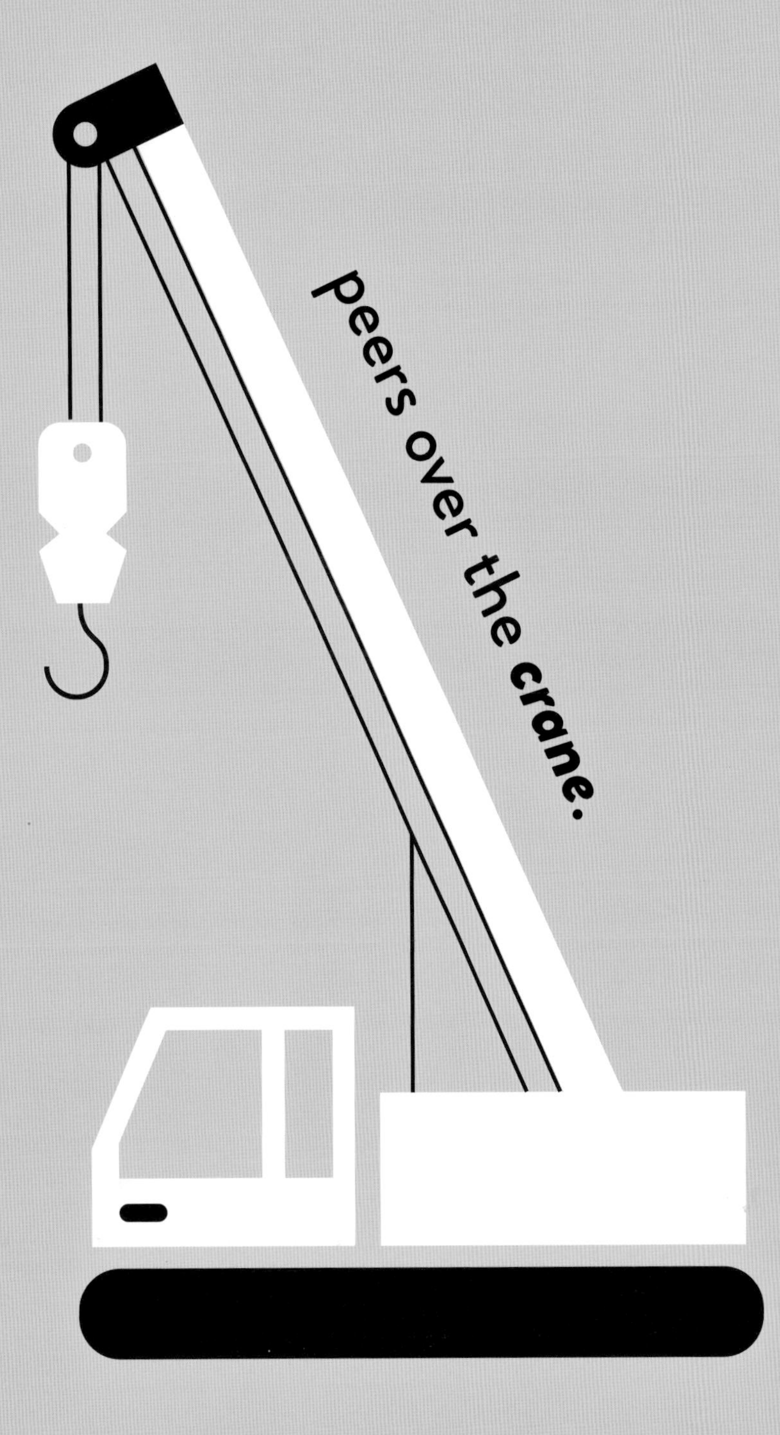

peers over the **crane.**

The greedy ***moose***

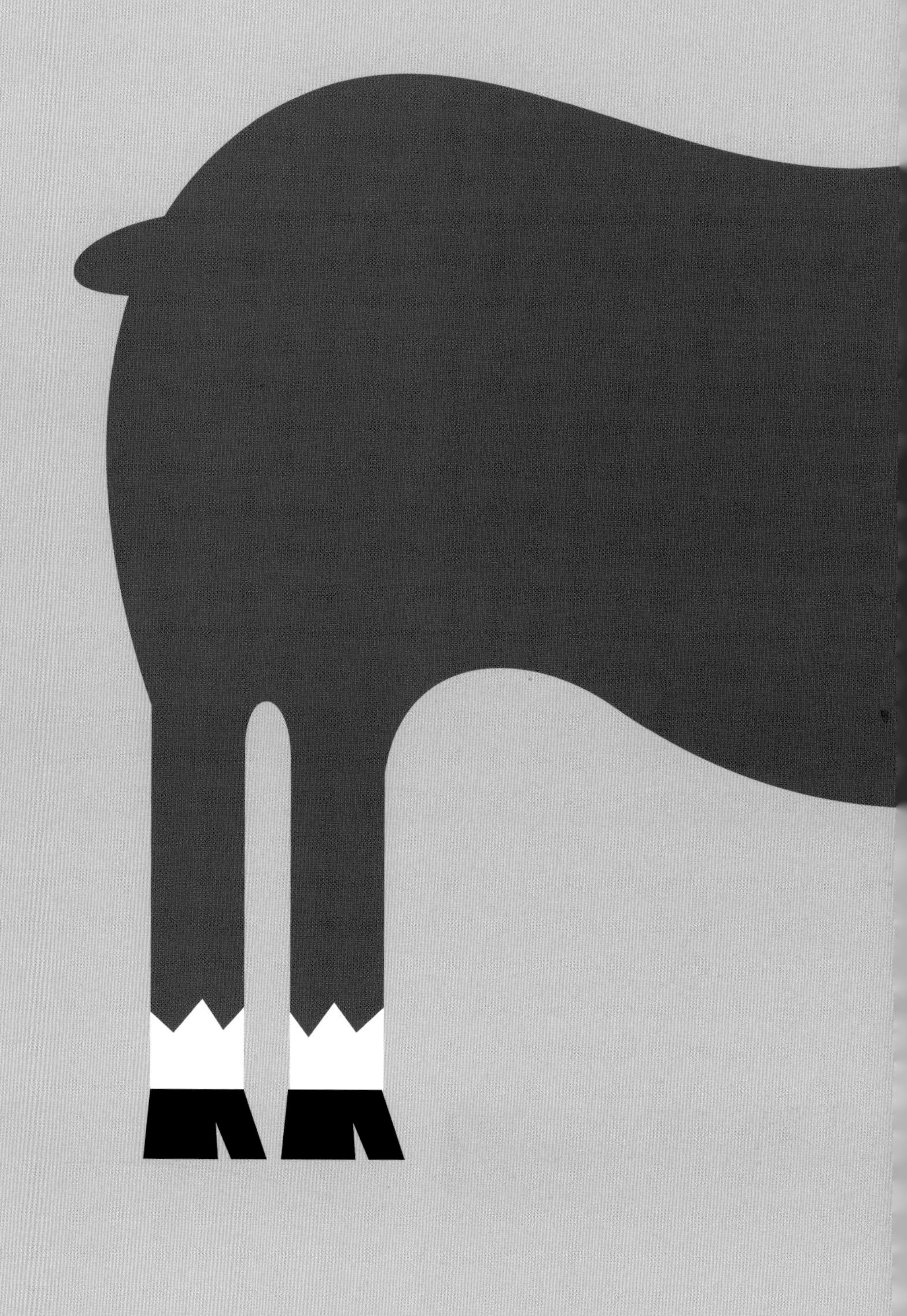

loves chocolate ***mousse.***

And the ***bear*** . . .

is ***bare***!

“The tall *duck* has to *duck*.”

Words that sound the same and are ***spelled the same*** but have different meanings are called ***homonyms***.

“And the *bear* is *bare*!”

Words that sound the same but are ***spelled differently*** and have different meanings are called ***homophones***.

LADYBIRD BOOKS

UK | USA | Canada | Ireland | Australia
India | New Zealand | South Africa

Ladybird Books is part of the Penguin Random House group of companies
whose addresses can be found at global.penguinrandomhouse.com
www.penguin.co.uk www.puffin.co.uk www.ladybird.co.uk

First published 2019
001

Printed in China

A CIP catalogue record for this book is available from the British Library

ISBN: 978-0-241-31203-2

All correspondence to:
Ladybird Books, Penguin Random House Children’s, 80 Strand, London WC2R 0RL